INSIDE

Little Brother BOOKS

Published 2020.
Little Brother Books, Ground Floor, 23 Southernhay East, Exeter, Devon, EX1 1QL
Printed in Poland.
books@littlebrotherbooks.co.uk | www.littlebrotherbooks.co.uk

The Little Brother Books trademarks, logos, email and website addresses and the GamesWarrior logo and imprint are sole and exclusive properties of Little Brother Books Limited.

This is an unofficial and independently written book, the inclusion of any logos, images, quotes and references does not imply endorsement. Whilst every care has been taken in researching and writing this book, due to the nature of the subject matter, some information may change over time.

Fortnite is a registered trademark of Epic Games. The screenshots and artwork shown in this guide were taken from Fortnite in game screenshots, a game created and published by Epic Games. This is a 100% unofficial and independent guide, which is in no way licensed, authorised or endorsed by or otherwise connected in anyway with Epic Games or any other individuals from Epic Games and authors of Fortnite. All copyrights and trademarks are recognised and used specifically for the purpose of criticism, review and reportage.

FORTNITE: A BRIEF HISTORY

IT'S HARD TO BELIEVE, BUT WHEN FORTNITE FIRST LAUNCHED (IN SEPTEMBER 2017), THERE WAS NO BATTLE ROYALE MODE AT ALL! THE GAME, WHICH HAD BEEN BRAINSTORMED BY EPIC GAMES TO IN-CORPORATE MINECRAFT-STYLE BUILDING INTO A SHOOTING GAME, HAD DONE REASONABLY WELL BUT NOT BRILLIANTLY.

When the free to play Battle Royale mode dropped in, all that changed. You could play against people on different consoles, and the colourful cartoon-style graphics meant younger gamers could get a shooting fix without loads of blood and gore.

In just two weeks, Fortnite gathered TEN MILLION players. By November 2017, it was TWENTY MILLION! A new gaming phenomenon was here,

and people quickly started to take notice. Fortnite's status as one of the biggest games in the world was confirmed in March 2018, when rapper Drake joined rising Fortnite star Tyler 'Ninja' Blevins on Twitch. At one point, 628,000 people were all watching at the same time – a new Twitch record!

In those early months, Fortnite changed quite quickly as Epic realised that the key to keeping people interested was to add more cool things to

play with. The first season was very basic, with only one icon and glider available to be earned, but Season 2 saw an important change as emotes were introduced – and the Fortnite world started dancing!

Season 3 saw the Battle Pass introduced and a lot more changes started to happen regularly. A meteor destroyed Dusty Depot on the map, the first change to the map – something we've now all become very used to as Fortnite changes the island from one season to the next.

The next landmark was the first live event, a rocket launch in Season 4, and the island also saw its first vehicle – the famous shopping cart! In fact, the summer of 2018 saw all kinds of important developments for Fortnite, including something that has become an integral part of the game – a tie-in with another franchise. That honour went to the Avengers with a Thanos and Infinity Stone link-up. Both Marvel and Epic said at the time that it wasn't a commercial deal but something that happened because they both loved each other's work – but Fortnite has certainly made the most of big tie-ins since!

FORTNITE'S COOLEST TIE INS

HERE ARE SOME OF THE COOLEST TIE-INS THAT FORTNITE HAS ENJOYED OVER THE YEARS – WE WONDER WHO WILL BE NEXT?

MARVEL AVENGERS

The first massive collaboration with another brand in Fortnite was the link-up with Avengers for Avengers: Endgame. As well as allowing players to take on the role of Thanos, there were also plenty of Avengers-themed weapons in the game, ranging from Captain America's shield to Thor's hammer. ⬆

JOHN WICK

John Wick was already a hugely popular figure in Fortnite, with an early skin seemingly very closely based on the character made famous by Keanu Reeves. It was little surprise then, when Epic went the whole hog and made things official. It began with one of Epic's beloved teasers – John Wick's house appearing in Paradise Palms. Before long, it was followed by an official skin and a game mode that allowed Fortnite players to work as bounty hunters – cool or what? ⬇

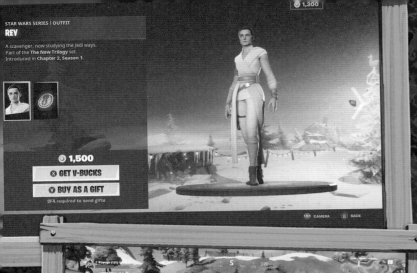

STAR WARS SERIES | OUTFIT
REV
A scavenger, now studying the Jedi ways.
Part of the **The New Trilogy** set.
Introduced in **Chapter 2, Season 1**.

Ⓒ 1,500
Ⓧ GET V-BUCKS
Ⓨ BUY AS A GIFT
2FA required to send gifts

STAR WARS

With The Rise of Skywalker arriving in cinemas, Fortnite fans were incredibly excited about a live event featuring a minute-long clip of the new film, along with a broadcast from Emporer Palpatine. What was truly mindblowing is that the broadcast from the Emperor was referenced in the movie but not actually heard. That means it's possible that LucasArts has made Fortnite part of Star Wars canon – that the Fortnite universe exists alongside the Star Wars one! If that's not worth geeking out over, we don't know what is!

As if that wasn't enough excitement, there were also Star Wars skins (which still crop up in the item shop from time to time) and the awesome lightsaber became available (probably a bit over-powered but it's still super exciting whenever it crops up in the game!) There was also a crashed Imperial craft on the island, guarded by Stormtroopers. If you killed them, you could take their laser blasters!

DEADPOOL

With his sarcastic one-liners and great put-downs, Deadpool seems a natural choice for a Fortnite appearance and so it proved in Chapter 2 when the cheeky so and so dropped into the game. The challenges based around Deadpool were suitably silly, including saluting his underpants and celebrating his love of partying by putting him on a swanky yacht.

LB PLAY BATTLE PASS COMPETE **LOCKER** ITEM SHOP CAREER V-BUCKS RB

Ⓒ 2,050

(UNSAVED)

Random

Ⓧ SAVE PRESET
Ⓨ RD CHANGES (H

OUTFIT MARVEL SERIES
DEADPOOL

FORTNITE CONCERTS

The idea that an artist would host a concert inside a videogame seemed totally crazy just a couple of years ago, but Fortnite is playing a big role in changing that opinion. Things were set in motion by Marshmello, who was already a huge Fortnite fan and so felt like 'one of our own'. He took part in the first Fortnite charity pro-am tournament so when he aired a pre-recorded concert in Fortnite, everyone stopped killing each other and came together to enjoy the moment. It worked for Marshmello too, gaining lots of new followers into the bargain!

Travis Scott was the next artist to take on the challenge of throwing a live gig in Fortnite. A stage appeared in Sweaty Sands a week or so before the live event, and Scott then performed five times, to make sure people all around the world could tune in at a sensible time for them.

To call it a success is an understatement – in total, almost 30 MILLION people attended the concerts, which saw Scott drop a brand new tune and, like Marshmello before him, pick up a considerable number of new fans and followers into the bargain!

KINGSMAN

A very small tie-in but that's what makes it even cooler – it's like a wicked easter egg more than a full-on collaboration. The inclusion of the Kingsman Umbrella as a weapon is a nice touch. As well as doing some immense damage as a melee weapon, it can also be used as a shield to absorb bullets, and it can even be used as a mini glider if you leap from a high point (though it's not perfect and you may still take some damage). Very cool though!

WHAT'S NEXT?

Whether you love the tie-in events or loathe them, one things for sure – they're here to stay. While there are no firm plans announced for what the future holds, we think there'll certainly be more collaborations with big franchises like Marvel and Disney. More Star Wars events seem inevitable, but it's the concerts and music performances that we think we'll see much more of in the future – which bands would you like to see rocking out on stage in Fortnite soon? Keep your eyes peeled, because it might just happen!

FORTNITE JARGON EXPLAINED!

IF YOU'RE NEW TO FORTNITE (AND EVEN IF YOU'RE NOT!) A LOT OF THE LANGUAGE USED BY PLAYERS IN THE GAME CAN BE CONFUSING. THAT'S WHERE THIS LITTLE GUIDE COMES IN – ALL OF THE SLANG PHRASES USED BY FORTNITE GAMERS EXPLAINED SO YOU NEED NEVER LOOK LIKE A NOOB AGAIN!

WHAT THEY SAY / WHAT THEY MEAN!

WHAT THEY SAY	WHAT THEY MEAN!
AR, Regular AR	Normal Assault Rifle
Bandies	Bandages
Bots	A term for someone who isn't very good at the game and plays as if they are computer controlled
Bubble	What some players call the storm circle – ie 'head to the bubble quickly, the storm is closing in!'
Bush Campers	Players who hide in bushes
Campers	Players who hide in one spot for as long as possible
Chuggie, Chugs	Chug Jug (though some players also use this to refer to slurpies!)
Crossie	Crossbow
Double Pumping	Placing two pump action shotguns in adjoining positions in your inventory so you can get two shots off quickly.
Half-pod	A potion that will give you 50% shield.
Heals	Any item that increases armour or health. 'You got any heals' means someone is asking if you have any items that can help them be tougher to eliminate
HUD	This stands for Heads-Up Display, and refers to all the things you can see on your screen. It includes the map in the top right, your weapons in the bottom right, the compass, the information feed telling you who has eliminated who and so on
Knocked	Taking an enemy down without killing them in squads or duos
Legendary SCAR	Epic or Legendary Assault Rifle
Loot Bait	The practice of leaving lots of loot on display, then hiding nearby and waiting for someone to come and try to collect it all
Minis	Mini shield
Nerfed	Refers to when Epic Games make a weapon weaker to even out the gameplay. For example: 'the minigun has been nerfed'
N00b/Noob	Someone who is new to the game – and usually not playing it very well, by making basic mistakes
No-skin	This refers to players using the default outfits. It CAN signal a new player, but often advanced players use no-skins to trick opponents into thinking they are new players.
OP	Over Powered. This means a weapon or vehicle is just too strong, giving players an unfair advantage
Res	Resuscitate – if a team mate calls 'res me' it means they need you to revive them quickly!
Shield Pop	Destroying an opponent's shield, leaving them vulnerable to further damage
Slurpie	Slurp Juice
Storm Troopers	Players who hide in the storm to avoid opponents shooting them
Supped	Suppressed – so a 'supped pistol' is a supressed pistol
Taccie	Tactical Shotgun
Turtling	Building a 1x1 cube with a roof on to heal inside, or to use to snipe from
Vaulted	Epic Games constantly change the weapons available in the game, taking some away only to bring them back later. Items that have been removed from the game have said to be 'vaulted'
XP	This is an abbreviation for 'Experience Points'. Increasing your XP helps you move through the rankings in Fortnite, unlocking new items as you go (if you have a Battle Pass)

LOOK THE PART!

ONE OF THE BEST PARTS IN FORTNITE IS *PERFECTING YOUR LOOK*, AND CHOOSING A SKIN THAT SUITS THE TYPE OF IMAGE YOU WANT TO PORTRAY. THERE ARE HUNDREDS TO CHOOSE FROM, SO WE'VE COMPILED A LIST OF SOME OF OUR FAVOURITES HERE FOR YOU. THERE'S SOMETHING FOR EVERY BUDGET, FROM THE UNCOMMON OUTFITS ALL THE WAY UP TO LEGENDARY, BUT REMEMBER – THERE'S NO ACTUAL ADVANTAGE TO BE GAINED OTHER THAN LOOKING COOL!

UNCOMMON (800)

BIRDIE

Type: Uncommon // **Cost:** 800 V-Bucks

She may look like she just stepped off the golf course, but Birdie is packing something a lot more lethal than a nine-iron in her backpack! If you see her leaping out of the bushes with a shotgun in her hands, you can be sure she isn't looking for someone to play golf with. FORE!

CLASH

Type: Uncommon // **Cost:** 800 V-Bucks

One of the newer skins from Chapter 2, Clash is the kind of kid your parents probably warn you about hanging out with. Mean and moody but with cool pink hair, you certainly wouldn't find us messing with her.

GRIT

Type: Uncommon // **Cost:** 800 V-Bucks

With a cool mask and jet black outfit, we think that Grit is one of the coolest skins available in the Uncommon category. Choose this skin and you'd better live up the name, showing the grit and determination to outlast your rivals.

PATHFINDER

Type: Uncommon // **Cost:** 800 V-Bucks

Come with us back to the very early days of Fortnite! Pathfinder might not look like the most exciting of skins, but she does represent a little bit of gaming history, dating back to the VERY FIRST season of Fortnite. Cool, huh!

SCOUT

Type: Uncommon // **Cost:** 800 V-Bucks

Just like Pathfinder, Scout is another look back to the early days of Fortnite. A simple yet classic design, Scout was first available all the way back in Season 1, so if you're a fan of nostalgia (and want to look like you've been in on the game since the very start) then look no further!

WHISTLE WARRIOR

Type: Uncommon // **Cost:** 800 V-Bucks

What better way to call foul on an opponent than by leaping out from behind your cover wearing an American Football referee's outfit? With this lady, there's no yellow or red cards – just the business end of a shotgun to punish you for your sins...

ARCTIC ASSASSIN

Type: Rare // **Cost:** 1,200 V-Bucks

BRRRR! Bit chilly out wouldn't you say? Not that it bothers Arctic Assassin. She's an old face to Fortnite fans, dating back to Season 1, and she is designed to blend into the snowy mountain ranges seamlessly. Less effective against a green forest though. Oh well, can't have it all.

SEA WOLF

Type: Rare // **Cost:** 1,200 V-Bucks

Avast ye land lubbers! This salty sea dog is after a lot more than buried treasure – he's after your very life! Part of the Scallywags set from series 8, he's best used on the water for extra pirate points, striking fear into the heart of your opponents!

FENNIX

Type: Rare // **Cost:** 1,200 V-Bucks

Okay, so fox hunting might be a cruel sport, but isn't it about time the foxes turned the tables? Well, thanks to this foxy skin, you can do just that. Looking cool in a turquoise jump suit, it's about time the humans find out what it's like to be hunted...

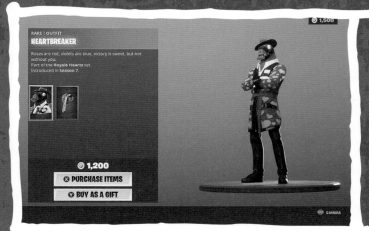

HEARTBREAKER

Type: Rare // **Cost:** 1,200 V-Bucks

Given the name, you're probably expecting some handsome hunk or gorgeous babe, right? Wrong. Heartbreaker is a llama. Whether he/she is an attractive llama or an ugly llama is probably a question you should never ask out loud.

HUGO

Type: Rare // **Cost:** 1,200 V-Bucks

Part of the spy set from Chapter 2, Season 2, Hugo is the kind of guy who'll park his car in a disabled bay right outside the party, win a fortune on the roulette table and then walk out with the girl you had your eye on all night. But when you're this smooth, who cares?

METAL MOUTH

Type: Rare // **Cost:** 1,200 V-Bucks

One of the coolest skins from Chapter 2, Season 1, Metal Mouth is clad head-to-toe in black, making him hard to spot in the shadows. The scary mask gives nothing away, but the truth is no-one lives long enough to find out what he looks like up close...

TOXIC TAGGER

Type: Rare // **Cost:** 1,200 V-Bucks

Tagging in Fortnite is one of the coolest parts of the game, though it seems fewer players bother these days. Toxic Tagger is here to change all that. Looking cool with his spray paint and hoody, he looks like he's just finished drawing glasses and a moustache on Banksy's latest effort.

ZADIE

Type: Rare // **Cost:** 1,200 V-Bucks

From the same set as Metal Mouth, there is no hiding from the fact that Zadie is every bit as creepy. In fact, she might even be creepier than her counterpart. If she leaps out of the shadows, you'll be too busy running away to even think about getting your shotgun out!

EPIC (1,500)

BEEF BOSS

Type: Epic // **Cost:** 1,500 V-Bucks

With his rather striking look, Beef Boss is one of the more recognisable skins from Fortnite – he even has his own action figure! If you love burgers (who doesn't?) then this is the skin for you – your opponents certainly won't be back for seconds.

BIG CHUGGUS

Type: Epic // **Cost:** 1,500 V-Bucks

One of the most-loved (and feared) Fortnite skins, Big Chuggus lives up to his name. Just look at those arms – enough to pick up an unsuspecting foe and fling them to an early doom from the highest of heights!

CLOAKED SHADOW

Type: Epic // **Cost:** 1,500 V-Bucks

There's something more than a little bit ominous about this rather scary chap. Dressed like an ancient religious figure, you definitely get the feeling he knows what the afterlife looks like – and can't wait to send you there to find out for yourself!

DOMINION

Type: Epic // **Cost:** 1,500 V-Bucks

Eek! When the devil himself comes calling, you know it really is the end of the road! With his satanic horns and terrifying red flesh, Dominion is not a man to be messed with. Use this skin if you like to see your enemies quaking in their boots as you bear down on them.

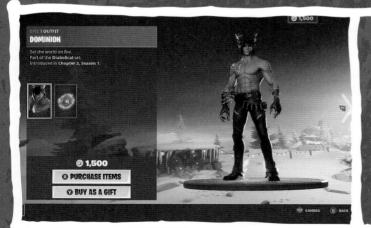

DREAMFLOWER

Type: Epic // **Cost:** 1,500 V-Bucks

Far out man! Why does everyone in Fortnite have to look so violent, when peace and flower power are so much cooler? Dreamflower is a spaced out hippy on the run from 70s-era San Francisco but don't be fooled, she'll still shotgun you in the face in heartbeat.

HIGHLAND WARRIOR

Type: Epic // **Cost:** 1,500 V-Bucks

Hmm. This character reminds us of a certain ice princess from a Disney movie. She won't bring snow to the island, however, but she will bring madness and mayhem from a mini machine gun. All together now: Let it go, let it gooooooo...

MECHA TEAM LEADER

Type: Epic // **Cost:** 1,500 V-Bucks

A flashback to one of the less popular phases in Fortnite history, the end of Season 9. This outfit is based on the Mecha from the end of Season 9, but try to forget about battles with over-powered Mechas – this is just a seriously cool skin.

WHITEOUT

Type: Epic // **Cost:** 1,500 V-Bucks

Another outfit that will see you blending into the snow but stick out like a sore thumb in the forest, Whiteout really does remind us of the star of a certain TV car show. We're not saying she IS the Stig, but they've never been seen in the same room...

REY

Type: Star Wars // **Cost:** 1,500 V-Bucks

The last Jedi in the universe, the big question is can Rey be the last combatant standing on the Fortnite island? This skin was part of the awesome Star Wars tie-in to coincide with the return of The Last Jedi, but she still makes occasional appearances in the shop.

LEGENDARY (2,000)

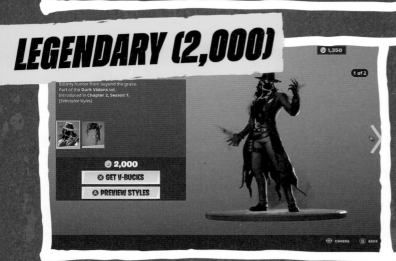

DEADEYE

Type: Legendary // **Cost:** 2,000 V-Bucks

If you're one of those people that can't decide if bounty hunters are cooler than zombies, then why not play as Deadeye? He's the best of both worlds – a truly creepy skin with a soul as black as his outfit.

DJ BOP

Type: Legendary // **Cost:** 2,000 V-Bucks

Everyone loves a teddy bear, don't they? Especially a teddy bear that loves to party! That might not be the case with DJ Bop, however. She looks friendly enough until the shooting starts, and all the glitterballs in the world won't stop her coming for you.

LEVIATHAN

Type: Legendary // **Cost:** 2,000 V-Bucks

The name sounds scary, but the reality – well, how scary can a little fish controlling a spaceman's body actually be? As well as looking completely bonkers, Leviathan is a cannibal, happily gulping down fishy treats from the waters around the island. The weirdo.

MOISTY MERMAN

Type: Legendary // **Cost:** 2,000 V-Bucks

Dating from way back in Season 4, Moisty Merman is another firm Fortnite favourite. Now that there is water to swim in on the island, there's no feeling quite like leaping out of a river to dispatch a couple of opponents before heading back to your watery haven.

OMEN

Type: Legendary // **Cost:** 2,000 V-Bucks

Another blast from the past, Omen has been creeping Fortnite players out since Season 4. A dark and sinister bad guy, he looks like he knows something you don't. Perhaps it's where to find all the legendary weapons hidden in the game. Let's hope not.

HARLEY QUINN

Type: DC Series // **Cost:** 2,000 V-Bucks

Everyone's favourite dysfunctional comic-book character is a Fortnite fave who pops up from time to time in the shop. She's as kooky as she is scary, and definitely not someone you want to get on the wrong side of...

HOW TO INCREASE YOUR XP

IF YOU WANT TO CLIMB TO THE TOP OF THE TREE AND UNLOCK ALL THE EXTRAS THAT COME WITH A BATTLE PASS, THEN THIS GUIDE TO BOOSTING YOUR XP WILL HAVE YOU REACHING LEVEL 100 IN NEXT TO NO TIME!

BATTLE PASS

The quickest way to increase your XP is to fork out your hard-earned pocket money for a Battle Pass. You can buy XP as part of the package, boosting your level into the bargain. It costs V-Bucks but remember that it's actually possible to earn enough V-Bucks by reaching level 100 with a Battle Pass to pay for your next Battle Pass (as long as you don't blow anything on crazy skins, emotes and weapon wraps, obvs). That means it's actually quite a sensible way to approach boosting your XP – and the higher your ranking, the more XP you'll gain.

RACK UP THE MEDALS

The medals system was new for Chapter 2, and they reset every day. Focus on hitting the achievements that unlock extra XP – surviving deep into the game so you get survivor medals, for example. They aren't worth loads of XP, but because you can earn them every day, they can help contribute to your overall total!

COMPLETE CHALLENGES

You should also regularly scroll through active challenges. Some of these are really easy to target – opening a set number of loot chests or ammo boxes in a specific location, for example. Identify those that are the most straightforward, and get them done quickly to help you increase your XP quicker. Often you can get a huge amount of XP just for landing in a specific location because doing so completes a challenge – perfect!

DAILY CHALLENGES

As well as the long-term challenges, there are often daily challenges that are around for 24 hours only. You need to log in every day to see them, and you can have three active at any time. Make sure you log in as often as possible (even if you don't have time to play) so that you can grab the daily challenge and store it for later! These are usually quite specific – eliminating two opponents with a shotgun, for example.

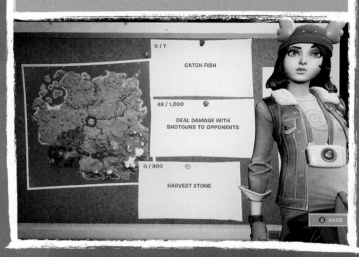

LOOK OUT FOR DOUBLE XP DAYS

Sometimes the Fortnite gods just smile on you. Keep an eye out for times when the guys and girls at Epic Games offer XP boosts on specific days. With an XP boost on, it's possible to really start flying though the rankings so check regularly.

HUNT DOWN XP COINS

Around the map you'll find XP coins. Running into these will earn you a quick XP boost. Green XP coins will just give you the coins straight away, while purple ones will break into smaller coins that you then have to chase down — but be quick, as they disappear after a few seconds!

PLAY SQUADS AND DUOS WITH NOOBS!

This is a bit cheeky, but if you have friends who are new to Fortnite, a great way to boost your (and their) XP is to play squads or duos with them. The reason is that the game will match you with players of a similar quality, so it's quite likely you will be in games with lots of other new players too. You can then put the extra experience you already have to good effect, and should find it easier to last long into the game and possibly even rack up a few wins more than you would normally be able to expect!

PARTY ASSIST

On the same basis as playing squads with noobs, you can use party assist so that the whole team gains XP for specific achievements. However, you need to focus on one achievement at a time, so you need to agree with your friends which challenge you will attempt, and then focus on getting it done.

A great example for this is a challenge such as opening seven chests in a specific location. Playing solo can make that hard because once you've landed and opened a couple of chests, you might find other players have landed in the same area and opened the others. However, if your whole squad descends on a location and you EACH open two or three chests, then the challenge will be completed almost instantly and you'll all be enjoying that sweet XP boost!

Note that party assist is sometimes removed for a season or two for a variety of reasons, but it's always worth checking to see if it is operational whenever you play squads or duos!

OPEN SESAME!
(ACTUALLY, OPEN EVERYTHING!)

One of the simplest things to do in the game will also earn you XP – opening loot chests and ammo boxes. Leave nothing empty, ever! Even if you have the perfect loadout, open any loot chests you can, and don't overlook ammo boxes either.

STAYING ALIVE

It sounds obvious, but don't forget that staying alive until the final few storm circles and eliminating opponents are great ways to boost XP too. Getting a few kills and staying into the game until the later stages are useful XP boosting tactics, especially when you combine a few other activities along the way.

MANAGING YOUR V-BUCKS

V-BUCKS IS THE FORTNITE CURRENCY THAT ENABLES YOU TO BUY BATTLE PASSES, EMOTES, SKINS, WEAPONS WRAPS AND MORE – BUT JUST LIKE REAL MONEY, YOU NEED TO MANAGE YOUR FINANCES CAREFULLY IF YOU WANT TO BE ABLE TO BUY ALL THE THINGS YOU WANT! HERE ARE SOME TOP TIPS!

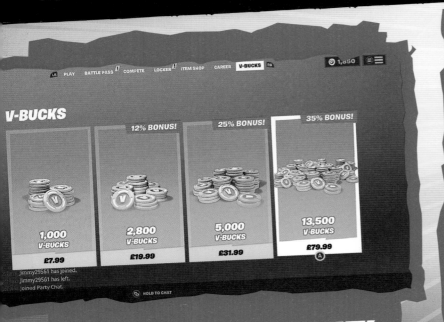

BATTLE PASS

If it's value for money you want, buying a Battle Pass is the smartest way to invest your V-Bucks. As you progress through the levels, you'll unlock loads of skins, wraps, sprays and emotes – far more than you would be able to afford if you were spending the money on buying them direct from the store. What's more, you'll also earn FREE V-Bucks as you move up the rankings. In fact, if you reach level 100 you'll find you'll have earned enough V-Bucks to buy a Battle Pass for the next season – which means you'll be able to keep going and do it all over again!

SAVE UP YOUR MONEY

The more V-Bucks you buy at the same time, the better value you tend to get overall, so play smart. If you have a sensible monthly limit that you can afford to spend on V-Bucks – perhaps your pocket money, or money you earn from chores or a part-time job – then it can make more sense to save it up for a while. Then, when you upload it all at the same time, you'll get more V-Bucks for less money.

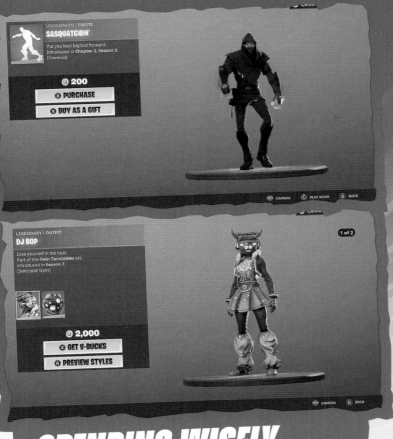

UNCOMMON | EMOTE
SASQUATCHIN'

Put your best bigfoot forward.
Introduced in Chapter 2, Season 2.
[Traversal]

🪙 200

❌ PURCHASE
❌ BUY AS A GIFT

CAMERA   PLAY AGAIN   BACK

LEGENDARY | OUTFIT
DJ BOP
1 of 2

Lose yourself in the beat.
Part of the Twin Turntables set.
Introduced in Season 7.
[Selectable Styles]

🪙 2,000

❌ GET V-BUCKS
❌ PREVIEW STYLES

CAMERA   BACK

V-Bucks

Buy 10,000 Fortnite (+3,500 Bonus) V-Bucks, the in-game currency that can be spent in Fortnite Battle Royale, Creative, and Save the World modes. In Battle Royale and Creative you can use V-Bucks to purchase new customization items like Outfits, Gliders, Pickaxes, Emotes, and the latest season's Battle Pass! In the Save the World co-op PvE mode, you can use V-Bucks to purchase X-Ray Llamas that contain weapon and trap schematics, plus new Heroes, and more! V-Bucks can be purchased in packs of various amounts, and you'll receive bonus V-Bucks when you buy packs of 2,500 V-Bucks or larger.

10,000 + 3,500
V-Bucks   BONUS
£79.99

❌ PURCHASE

V-BUCKS ON DIFFERENT CONSOLES

Although you can play Fortnite on different machines, your V-Bucks will only be available on the format you bought them on. Once you've bought something, you can use it on your account whatever you use to play Fortnite, but unspent V-Bucks need to be spent on the same format that you bought them on. Don't buy V-Bucks while logged into your mobile phone account and think you can spend them later on your PS4 – you won't be able to!

SPENDING WISELY

Like in all shops, there's something to suit all budgets in Fortnite! There are different grades to the outfits, harvesting tools, weapon wraps, gliders and so on that you can buy. The system matches that used for weapons, so you have common, uncommon, rare, epic and legendary. The higher the ranking of the goodies you want to buy, the more you need to spend!

AVOID SCAMS AND SCAMMERS

The most important thing to bear in mind is that there is no legitimate way to get V-Bucks outside the game itself. A quick google will uncover lots and lots of websites offering ways to earn V-Bucks but don't fall for it – they're all cons. Entering credit or debit cards into any other site outside of Fortnite itself will not earn you V-Bucks, and could see your details (or your parents' details) stolen and defrauded. Epic Games will never message you and ask for your login details either, so don't fall for any of the tricks out there – stay safe online, and keep your hard-earned V-Bucks for yourself!

50 LEVEL FARMER DEATHRUN   **CELEBRATE STAR WARS**

STAR WARS OUTFITS RETURN

The Rey, Kylo Ren, and Sith Trooper Outfits are back for a limited time. Grab a lightsaber to celebrate! May the 4th be with you.

CHECK IT OUT   CLOSE

DON'T DELAY – BUY TODAY!

Most of the items available in the store will be there for one day only and then disappear for a while – often a very long time! If you see something you really want and you have the V-Bucks to buy it, you need to decide quickly or you could be left kicking yourself!

ITS ONLY COSMETIC

It's important to remember that the things you can buy in Fortnite look cool – but that's all they do. You won't be gaining a competitive advantage by having a particular skin or glider, so you don't NEED to buy anything at all to be a great Fortnite player!

TACTICS: CLOSE QUARTERS COMBAT

A LOT OF THE FIGHTING YOU'LL BE DOING IN FORNITE WILL BE UP CLOSE AND PERSONAL. THERE ARE LOTS OF BUILDINGS TO EXPLORE, AND OPPONENTS COULD BE LURKING ROUND ANY CORNER – SO YOU NEED TO MAKE SURE YOU'RE PREPARED FOR ANY EVENTUALITY!

SHOT SELECTION

When things get up close and personal, it's best to switch to the right weapon for the job. Usually, that's going to be a shotgun or an SMG for the best results. If you have a tactical shotgun available, use that over anything that only fires one or two shots – being able to get a volley of shots off in quick succession is essential in a close-range firefight. ➡

WALK, DON'T RUN!

It's best to crouch when inside buildings and to walk rather than run. Running makes too much noise, and will alert anyone else inside the building to your presence. Instead, keep quiet and try not to draw attention to yourself! You can also find you are taken by surprise by running into an opponent and in that split second or two while you try to aim, it can be game over! ⬇

BE READY!

You're most likely to end up in close quarters combat when you are inside a building, so always be prepared when you enter one! Switch to an appropriate weapon, and make sure it is fully loaded. Changing weapon or reloading it makes a noise that can give your position away! ⬆

PACK SENSIBLY

Keep your close-range weapons together in your inventory. If you don't have a tactical shotgun you can hold two or three pump action shotguns in consecutive slots. Instead of reloading after each shot, simply change to the next weapon along. It's miles quicker than reloading and you can take most enemies down in three shots using this technique (it's still better to have a tactical shotgun or SMG though!) ⬆

FULL CLIP ACTION

If you are using an SMG at close range, there's not really much need to feather the trigger. It does lose accuracy if you just empty the whole magazine, but not enough to make much difference at close range. Just unload the whole clip into your opponent, but be sure to reload or switch to your next weapon quickly in case there's someone else nearby. ⬆

BODY SHOTS

Headshots may look cool on your replays, but there's always an increased risk of missing. At close range, aim for the torso – it's a bigger target to hit and if you aim slightly too high or slightly too low, you're still hitting something. ⬆

LORDS A-LEAPING

When using a shotgun, you need to get pretty close and that can give your opponent a free shot. The best way to negate that, if you can't sneak up on them from behind, is to jump. It's much easier to hit an opponent on the ground while you're in the air than it is for the grounded player to land a shot on someone leaping all over the place. This is also a useful tactic if you're forced to engage outside and only have a shotgun – jumping can help you close the distance on an opponent without getting hit, making it into the range you need to do damage. ⬆

MELEE MAYHEM

There are some melee weapons in the game – usually special ones like lightsabers or the Kingsman umbrella. Using them at close range can be deadly if you can deploy them before your opponent can fight back, so they are best combined with good old-fashioned stealth and cunning. Your harvesting tools are also a melee weapon but they only do 20 damage at a time and should only ever be used in the nightmare scenario of being in combat without having any weapons! ⬆

TACTICS: RANGED COMBAT

WHILE A LOT OF THE ACTION IN FORTNITE TAKES PLACE IN THE SETTLEMENTS AROUND THE ISLAND, YOU ALSO NEED TO BE COMFORTABLE *FIGHTING IN OPEN SPACES* AND ENGAGING OPPONENTS AT DISTANCE.

SHIELD YOURSELF

If you're running across an expanse of grass and a bullet whizzes past your head, your instinct is to turn towards it while you figure out where it came from. Your instincts will get you shot in Fortnite, however, so it's time to retrain yourself. Instead, get into the habit of IMMEDIATELY building a simple wall between you and the direction the shot came from. It need only be one or two sections long, and wood is absolutely fine. You're just buying yourself a couple of seconds to compose yourself, peek round the edge, and see where the danger is. ⬇

RIGHT WEAPON

When heading across open spaces, switch immediately to a weapon that's well suited to the task – ideally an assault rifle or burst assault rifle. If you come under fire, you'll want to be able to engage quickly without having to hunt around in your inventory first. ⬆

SNIPER RIFLES

Sniper rifles are incredibly powerful weapons that are usually one shot one kill. However, you need to be accurate and because they are single shot, you'll lose valuable time reloading. Sniper rifles are therefore best used when you are already IN position – perhaps in a hiding spot in a house, laid low on a roof or at the top of your own tower. Using them on the run while under fire is really tough and will often see you taken out first. They are best used when you have spotted an opponent and have a clear shot with no chance of coming under fire yourself. ➡

USE COVER

When shooting against an enemy at distance, use any available cover you can. Building walls yourself is one tactic, but make the most of any buildings you happen to be near. Duck behind them and then pop up on the other side – the key is to keep your opponent guessing where you'll fire from next and not to give them a free shot. ⬆

CHOOSE WHEN TO ENGAGE

Firing from a distance is risky, and it's even more risky if you are exposed. There's no guarantee you'll eliminate the opponent you are aiming at, and even if you do, you may just draw attention to yourself. As such, you should really only open fire when you're sure you can secure the elimination. Often, it's easier to try to close the distance on your opponent before opening fire to give yourself a better chance.

One thing you should be sure to avoid at all times is firing at an opponent who has cover while you are exposed. All you'll do is draw attention to yourself and allow your rival to take you down while making the most of the cover they already have. ⬆

I HAVE THE HIGH GROUND

It's always better to have the higher ground, so look to secure it whenever you can. Aiming down means you can see more of your opponent, while the curve of the rise means you can duck out of sight by simply taking a step or two backwards. ⬆

STAY LOW

From any kind of distance, accuracy is key. To give yourself the best chance of hitting the target, make sure you are looking down the weapon sights while also crouching low. This will give you a stable base from which to shoot and increases your accuracy. However, don't just stay still after taking a couple of shots – you'll need to be up quickly, move to another location and go again. ⬆

DON'T LOSE FOCUS

When you're engaged in a long-distance shoot-out, it's easy to forget there can be 98 other gamers as well as you and your opponent. Keep checking your immediate surroundings and

TACTICS: STATIC EXPLOSIVES

STATIC EXPLOSIVES REFERS TO EXPLOSIVES THAT YOU SET IN PLACE AND THEN DETONATE LATER. SOMETIMES THEY CAN BE VAULTED, BUT THERE IS USUALLY AT LEAST ONE FORM OF STATIC EXPLOSIVE AVAILABLE IN THE GAME – SO HERE'S HOW TO MAKE THE MOST OF THEM!

PROXIMITY MINES

These bad boys are great for planting near to areas you think will attract opponents. Pinch points on the way into or out of a building are one good example – but you can also plant them round loot chests to give anyone running in to grab some goodies a thoroughly nasty shock.

Another great use of proximity mines is to drop them if you're being chased. Should an opponent spot you and give chase, drop them just round a corner and wait for that sucker to sprint after you to their doom.

There's never an excuse not to use proximity mines. Even if you have a full inventory and don't want to carry them with you, deploy them and pick up something else. That way, if anyone does run past them later in the game, you'll still get the kill — something that's impossible if you just put them back on the floor without arming them.

REMOTE C4

Throw or drop this and then detonate it from a distance. You need to see your opponents in order to make this weapon useful. In the heat of a firefight, it's quite an ask to be able to throw them and then detonate them, so they are best off being used in a pre-planned way. Plant them near choke points or loot chests, then hide nearby. When an opponent gets close – **BOOM!**

Alternatively, these can be a useful way to take out enemies below you by dropping the remote charges down a hill or off the side of a building and detonating them.

Lastly, you can also use them to destroy defences – planting C4 on a wall and then detonating it to expose opponents who had been using it as cover, for example. This is an especially useful tactic to employ when competing in duos or squads, but it can also be pulled off successfully in solo mode.

ON THE MOVE

There's nothing to stop you using static explosives in a similar way to grenades – throwing them at opponents and then detonating them immediately. Doing so can be a little cumbersome though, so it's a tactic best used in emergencies only. ⬅

TACTICS: RANGED EXPLOSIVES

RANGED EXPLOSIVES ARE GREAT FUN – YOU THROW THINGS, THEY GO BANG. WHAT'S NOT TO LOVE? HERE ARE SOME OF THE WAYS THEY CAN HELP YOU COME OUT ON TOP IN COMBAT.

THROW DOWN – NEVER UP!

Because grenades often don't have the best range, and aiming them isn't the easiest, it's usually best to drop grenades down on enemies once you have secured the high ground. Trying to throw grenades at opponents who are up a hill is especially risky – aim short, and your grenade will come tumbling down the hill straight back at you! ⬇

TYPES OF RANGED EXPLOSIVES

The most frequent type of ranged explosives are grenades. The most important thing to remember about grenades is that they don't explode on impact – there are a few seconds after the grenade land before it will explode. That means getting the timing of your throw just right to cause maximum damage.

Rocket launchers are the other primary way to cause explosive damage to enemies from a distance – but the big weakness with them is that the rockets are incredibly slow, and they make a loud noise when they are fired – which warns your target about what's about to happen! ⬆

DESTROY BUILDINGS

You can pair up ranged explosives and use them in conjunction with your other weapons when it comes to attacking opponents who are using cover. Throw your grenades or fire your rocket at the cover, then switch to a gun and take them out as their cover is destroyed, or they attempt to flee to safety. ➡

THROW IN BUNCHES

Because it can take a while for grenades to detonate, your opponent will have a few seconds to escape, so use grenades in groups for the best chance of eliminating them. Grenades will normally be found in groups of three, and you can carry up to six in a single slot, so throw as many as you can in quick succession. The best technique is to aim one directly at your target, then one a few yards to the left and another a few yards to the right. As they try and flee the first grenade, they'll find themselves running towards the second. Then, as they turn to avoid the second grenade, they'll be running in the direction of the third. Crafty, eh? ⬇

UP CLOSE AND PERSONAL

Rocket launchers are SLOW. Using them against people from a distance is a waste of time because they'll have plenty of time to get out of the way and usually all you'll succeed in doing is giving away your own location. If you want to cause damage with a rocket launcher (and they will cause LOTS of damage with a direct hit) try to get within 10-20 metres of your opponent. At that range, they'll have less chance to escape. Don't aim directly for your opponent though – if you miss them, the rocket will just trundle off harmlessly into the distance. Instead, aim for the ground near their feet. The explosion will cause them a load of damage and probably eliminate them – but if you're too close, you'll cause significant damage to yourself.

Using a similar approach to aiming at the floor, you can also take out opponents if they are standing near a wall or cliff by aiming for that instead. Going for a direct hit is virtually impossible though, so don't even think about it. ⬆

DESTROYING STRUCTURES FROM A DISTANCE

One thing rockets can be used for from long range is to destroy structures – especially ones built by your opponents to defend themselves with. When playing in a duo or a squad, work together so that your team mate(s) get up close to the structure, then you destroy it from distance. Your buddies can then swoop in and mop up afterwards!

You can even use this trick in solo, if you see a battle between two opponents in the distance. Use your rocket launchers to help destroy any defensive structures so one of your opponents can eliminate the other! ➡

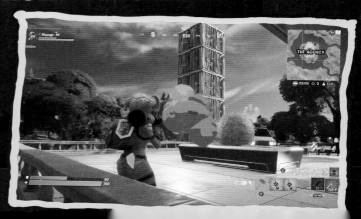

STAYING HEALTHY

IF YOU WANT TO LAST UNTIL THE END OF A BATTLE ROYALE, THEN YOU'LL NEED TO KNOW HOW BEST TO KEEP YOUR HEALTH AND SHIELD MAXED OUT FOR MINIMUM EFFORT! HERE ARE SOME GREAT WAYS TO MAKE SURE YOU KEEP AS STRONG AS POSSIBLE TO GIVE YOURSELF THE EDGE IN COMBAT!

WARM YOURSELF BY THE FIRE

Around the map you'll often encounter campfires. You can light these in order to restore your health back up to 100, and can heal quicker if you have harvested some wood to stoke the fire while you heal.

However, be careful. The camp fire will send smoke into the air, alerting nearby enemies to your location. It's a smart move to get away from the camp fire as soon as your health has recovered, before you get tracked down. Remember too that each campfire can only be lit once, so you can't return to campfires you have previously used if you need to heal again. ⬇

USING SLURP POTIONS

There are two types of slurp potions that can increase your shield – small potions and big potions. Small potions are worth 25 shield, while large potions are worth 50. However, small potions can't increase your shield past 50.

That means you have to be smart when it comes to using potions. If you have no shield and find a large potion, keep it in your inventory until you have found a couple of smaller potions to take you to 50. There's nothing more annoying than drinking a large potion to move to 50 shield, then finding two smaller ones that you can't use until you've taken damage!

Remember that drinking potions leaves you vulnerable, so always take cover. Bigger potions take longer to drink than smaller potions, and

FISHING

You can eat fish too, which will restore varying amounts of health! Catch them with one of the fishing rods you'll find near to the various bodies of water around the map. Simply look for spots in the water where there are ripples and cast your line to bag some healthy grub. You can also find fish hidden in fridges around the map too. ⬇

USING MEDKITS

Medkits operate in a similar way to slurp potions – smaller ones only repair you 15 health points, up to a maximum of 75 this time. Large medkits will restore you to 100 health however much damage you have taken, but they take a LONG time to administer – ten seconds in total. That means it's VITAL you only use them when you have found good cover. ⬆

SLURPY SWAMP

The owners of the Slurp factory aren't too fussed about the environment, but for once that's not a bad thing! The waters round Slurpy Swamp are infected with gloop, but that means that the water itself heals you. Simply jump in and you'll see your health and armour start to increase. Be careful, however – Slurpy Swamp is often a very busy landing spot for this very reason! ⬇

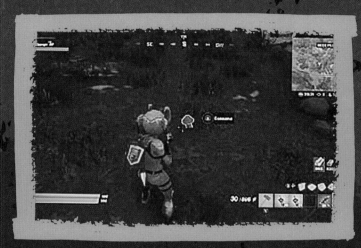

FORAGING FOR GOODIES

Around the map you'll often find little goodies you can eat that will repair your health or armour. These can change from one season to the next, but they include apples and mushrooms. They don't give you much health, but they can come in handy as you move from one area to another. ⬆

SLURP CANISTERS AND LORRIES

Dotted around the factory and outhouses of Slurpy Swamp are canisters containing slurpy goo. Use your harvesting tool to give these a good wallop. As well as the metal you'll harvest, you'll also find your health gets a boost too. If you find any Slurpy lorries, smashing them will send your energy zooming – along with anyone else nearby. Great news if you're in a squad and have all taken some damage! ⬅

SOLO TACTICS

IF YOU WANT TO BE THE LAST MAN STANDING WHEN IT COMES TO BATTLE ROYALE, YOU'LL NEED TO HAVE YOUR TACTICS ABSOLUTELY SPOT ON. GOOD JOB WE'RE HERE TO HELP YOU OUT THEN, ISN'T IT?

USE COVER

Wandering round the map without a care in the world will have you picked off in next to no time. The way to survive is to stay close to buildings and natural cover whenever possible, so that you are only vulnerable from attack in one or two directions. Wandering aimlessly through the fields is a one-way ticket to Eliminationville!

BIDE YOUR TIME

Don't draw attention to yourself by trying to take out enemies from long distance, unless you have the right weapons (especially a sniper rifle). Very often, all you will do is draw attention to your location and make yourself a sitting duck. Instead, try to sneak up on the opponent you have spotted. You really should not be firing unless and until you are completely sure you will be able to secure an elimination!

HARD TO HIT

For those times when it is impossible to avoid crossing an open expanse, make yourself as hard to hit as possible. Zig zag, jump, switch between sprinting and walking – do whatever you need to do to make sure anyone looking at you down the scope of a sniper rifle doesn't have a clue what you'll do next! Don't forget to spin round every so often to check there's no-one sneaking up on you either!

CROUCH AND FIRE!

You're more accurate when you are standing still and crouched down. Firing while moving too much (especially at distance) is counter-productive. Of course, you can't just stay still during a battle as you'll be taken out in no time, but where you can, stop, crouch, fire and THEN move to make yourself harder to hit. If you spot an opponent who doesn't know you're coming, crouching down will make you more accurate when you do decide to take the shot.

THE BEST YOU CAN GET

Always dump weapons for better versions of the same weapon. You can tell the difference by how many stars they have, but also the colour – grey, green, blue, purple, gold. Trade up in that order!

UPGRADE

Dotted around the map you'll find upgrade benches. These can be combined with the resources you have harvested to increase the quality of the weapon you are holding. However, use them wisely. There's little point in upgrading a one star weapon to two star, so save upgrades for your weapons that are already pretty near the top of the tree to give yourself a real advantage.

HARVEST EARLY

Later in the game, you'll be in a smaller area and the sound of you harvesting can give your location away. It also distracts you and makes you an easier target. Instead, if you're an avid builder, grab the things you need early on so that you've got a healthy reserve of materials for the latter stages of the game.

SIDEGRADE

As well as increasing the quality of a weapon, you can change its type at one of the benches. This usually costs fewer resources, and can give you a real competitive advantage. For example, an assault rifle can be converted into a heavy assault rifle that does more damage per shot, albeit with a slightly reduced magazine capacity.

HARVEST SMART

Always look to hit the weak point when harvesting. It's a little blue circle that pops up. Aiming for it will do extra damage so you'll harvest quicker, and can get back to holding a weapon instead of a pickaxe. No-one wants to be a sitting duck!

BUILDING

Building structures is often the difference between winning and losing. Mastering the art of construction is a crucial skill, especially when you have no team mates to help you. Practice, practice and practice until you can quickly get simple towers and walls in place with ease. It's a crucial technique to master, especially once you get into the latter stages of the game.

BEHIND A WALL

When you are shot at from a distance, it's natural to turn to face the direction of the shot and try and see who hit you. Doing so can often be lethal, as you may well find that the opponent who just missed you lands their next shot or two and its game over for you. Instead, make constructing a quick wall an instinctive reaction. As soon as you see a bullet zip past you, spin and build a wall between you and the direction it came from. Even if it's just a wooden wall a couple of sections long, it will buy you time to compose yourself, see where the shots are coming from, and form a plan – whether it's to escape or to return fire!

EYE ON THE STORM

It might sound obvious, but keep track of the storm circle. Being eliminated because you didn't realise how close the storm was and how far you are away from safety is dumb. Don't be dumb!

LISTEN UP!

If you've got headphones, use them! You can often hear opponents before you see them, especially inside buildings where their footsteps will give them away.

ARRANGE YOUR INVENTORY

Keep weapons in logical places in your allocated slots. It makes sense to have close-range weapons together and then longer-range weapons together, so that you can switch between weapons quickly in combat, especially if you run out of ammo. If you always use the same basic approach to your inventory, you'll find this easy. If you keep things in a random order, you'll distract yourself by constantly checking what is where, and that delay could be costly. There's nothing more annoying than running out of bullets and then lamely throwing a medkit at your opponent because your inventory is in a muddle...

DUO TACTICS

WORKING AS A PAIR MEANS YOU'LL BE ABLE TO DO SOME THINGS THAT ARE SIMPLY NOT POSSIBLE IN SOLO MODE, BUT YOU WON'T HAVE THE BENEFIT OF AS MANY TEAMMATES AS YOU DO IN SQUADS – SO A MIX OF STEALTH AND STRENGTH NEEDS TO BE ACHIEVED!

SHARING IS CARING

Remember your teammate when it comes to loot! While in solo mode it's understandable to grab all the best weapons you can, but in duos, you really need your teammate to be in a strong position too. Make sure you share out the loot items you find equally, so that you are both well-equipped to deal with any situation that comes up in a match. Make sure you both have close-range and long-range weapons so you're prepared for any eventuality – it's no good one of you having four shotguns and the other having four assault rifles because you just won't be able to work together. ⬇

COMMUNICATION IS KEY

With just two of you, you'll need to know exactly where your teammate is at all times, and the same will apply to them. Don't suddenly decide to search a building for loot chests without telling them. Use voice chat if you can to keep each other informed of what you are doing, and what's happening around you. ➡

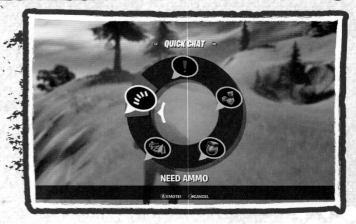

SPLIT MEDKITS AND POTIONS

If you are carrying a full medkit, then picking up more medkits will not take up further space in your inventory – you can carry up to three full medkits

or up to ten packs of bandages in the same slot. The same applies to large and small shield potions – three large shield potions will only occupy one slot, as will six smaller ones.

With that in mind, it makes more sense for each of you to only carry one type of heal item. That way, you can carry three full medkits and have four inventory slots free for weapons while your teammate can carry three full shield potions and still have four free inventory slots. It's more efficient than both of you carrying separate shield potions and medkits – you can just give each other items as required when it is safe to do so instead. ⬆

FOCUS YOUR FIRE

If you find yourself in combat with another duo, you should both focus your fire on the SAME opponent, rather than taking one each. Doing so means that opponent will take damage much quicker and be knocked to the ground – at which point you will outnumber the surviving player and can both focus your fire on them. That's a far more effective approach than wearing down two players equally because you'll still be coming under fire from two sets of weapons. Take down enemies one at a time in order to rule the world of Duos! ⬇

FINISHING FALLEN OPPONENTS

If you take an opponent to their knees, wait a while before finishing them off. They pose you no direct threat themselves, but rushing to finish them off might leave you at the mercy of their teammate, so only ever look to finish an opponent off if there's no immediate risk to you. However, it's often best to leave them alive. While they are knocked down, you can bet your bottom dollar their teammate will be thinking of a way to get to them and revive them, so you can lay a little trap.

Alternatively – and if you're sure there's no ambush waiting for YOU – get over to them and shake them down to reveal the location of their teammate so that you and your buddy can go and hunt them down! ⬇

COVER EACH OTHER

When it comes to building or harvesting, you should NEVER both be doing it at the same time. It leaves you as sitting ducks for any other duos that find you. One of you should have a weapon equipped and cover the other while they build or harvest. ⬇

HELP YOUR TEAMMATE

When you are knocked down, you can still crawl so help your buddy out if you want them to revive you safely. Crawl towards them to save them time, or head inside a building so that they will have cover when they come to revive you. Don't just lie there in an open space – that's helping no-one! ⬆

SAFE REVIVAL

There are only two of you in Duos (the clue is in the name) so if your teammate is knocked down, EVERYTHING depends on you. It's absolutely essential that you don't fall into a trap by rushing straight in to revive them. Find out who hit them and from where, and make sure the area is safe before you move in. It might even be that you need to wait it out and use your teammate's reboot card instead of risking moving too quick for a revive.

If you need to revive in an open space, be sure to build a defensive structure around you both so that you have some cover – you'll be completely defenceless while you revive your fallen comrade. ⬆

CUT YOUR LOSSES AND RUN

Sometimes it's unavoidable – you have to leave your teammate and look after number one. There's no point in having you both eliminated while you try to wade through a blazing firefight to revive your buddy. On occasions, it's best to slink off into the distance and work alone to try and finish as high up the rankings as possible, so that you both benefit from the extra XP. ⬆

BUILDING TIPS

When building in duos, one key tip is not to share the same structure. If you're both perched at the top of a 1x1 tower, it's far too easy for another duo to take you both out at the same time with a well-placed explosives assault, for example. If you're both building, stay close enough to each other you can support each other, but not in the same structure – it's way too easy to be taken out like that! ⬇

TOGETHER FOREVER

Aside for the odd occasion when you might be flanking an opponent, you need to stay close together in duos. Not so close that a single explosive or volley of gunfire can take you both out, but close enough that you can support each other in a firefight. From the start, make sure you land in the same area and work as a team. ⬆

SQUAD TACTICS

WHEN PLAYING IN A GROUP OF FOUR, THERE ARE A FEW EXTRA TACTICS YOU CAN EMPLOY THAT ARE EITHER IMPOSSIBLE OR INEFFECTIVE WHEN PLAYING IN SOLO OR DUOS. MASTERING SOME OF THESE TECHNIQUES COULD BE THE DIFFERENCE BETWEEN *SUCCESS* AND *FAILURE!*

SQUAD TACTICS

From time to time there are vehicles in the game – these have been varied in the past, and included cars, motorboats and choppers. If you are playing squads, it's a great way to make the most of these – especially if you're airborne. There's no point in heading up in a chopper on your own, for example – but with three squadmates with you, you can rain lead from the skies on your opponents! Whichever vehicles are available to you, using them together is key – it's no good one of you running off alone to use it if they don't have the support of the others! ⬆

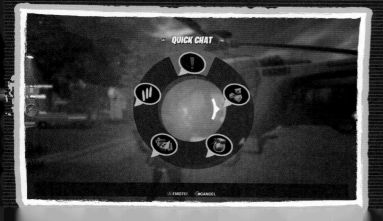

TALK TALK TALK!

Clear communication is the first step to being successful in squads. If you have a headset, use it! Call out what you are doing and where you are. If you're heading up the stairs, say so. If you're dropping excess weapons and goodies, tell your teammates. If you need something (like a medkit) then let them know. Communicating clearly and quickly can often be decisive, so make sure you use it to your advantage. Make the most of your time in the lobby while waiting for the game to start to outline your plans! ⬅

LAND IN PAIRS

If you're playing as a four, it's a good idea to land in pairs reasonably close to each other, rather than all four of you landing in exactly the same spot. That way you're close enough to each other to be able to offer support quickly, but not so close you can be surrounded and taken out right at the start of the game! ⬆

DEFENSIVE STRUCTURE

When the time is right to revive a teammate, carry them somewhere safe, such as in a building. If that's not an option, build a structure around yourself so you can heal your fallen comrade without someone taking a pot shot from distance. ⬇

DON'T GO FOR THE REVIVE

If you're in a firefight and one of your teammates is down, don't head straight over to revive them until the battle is over — just look after number one until the coast is clear. Reviving a teammate is a slow process and will leave you vulnerable, so it's not something to try and rush! ⬆

BUILD IN TURN

If you're building a fort or tower, then work as a group. Only have one or two people building at any one time, and have the others scanning the horizon and keeping them safe. You can rotate who is building and who is on lookout duty if you're constructing something big, so that everyone keeps a decent amount of resources in their inventory.

CLOSE - BUT NOT TOO CLOSE

Don't play as a lone wolf. It's way too easy for more organised squads to take you out if you are on your own. Instead, move together as a group, but don't stand too close to each other. If you're in a tight formation then a well-placed grenade or rocket launcher shot can take you all out, so make sure you're far enough apart. Think of it as sensible social distancing!

MEDIC!

Work as a group. Carrying lots of armour and medkits can take up valuable space in everyone's inventory, but making smart use of a bandage bazooka can be crucial. Get one of your crew to carry it along with three decent weapons. They can then heal their team mates between gun fights so you always have 100% health as a group. The bandage bazooka can be fired from distance so you can even operate from outside a battle, firing in medkits to your teammates as they take damage!

DIVIDE AND CONQUER

When you spot a group of enemies on the horizon, the best approach is to split up and try to outflank them. If you all attack in a single group, it's much easier for your opponents to take you out. Splitting into two pairs and attacking from opposite directions can work a treat. It can confuse your opponents and leave them unsure which threat to deal with first, making life easier for your squad!

DIVERSION TACTICS

Another great way to take down a group of opponents is to use a diversion. Sneak two players as close as possible to their location, ideally one on either side of the group, so you are lined up like the letter T, with two players at the bottom and one player on either side at the top. Then have the two players at the bottom open fire from distance. If it goes to plan, they'll draw the attention of the group and the two players who have snuck up on them can take them down from the sides! ⬆

STRAIGHT KNOCKOUT

If an opponent has teammates left in the game, they will fall to their knees when their health reaches zero, giving their teammates a chance to heal them. However, if an opponent dies immediately after you shoot them, it means they were the last remaining member of their squad so you can relax a little. That doesn't mean there isn't another squad lurking nearby, of course! ⬆

LOOK OUT FOR MULTIPLE ENEMIES

Remember, your opponents are in squads too! If you've taken one down, there may well be others nearby! For that reason, be wary about rushing over and looting fallen opponents straight away – you need to look out for their teammates! ⬇

A PICK-ME-UP

If you've knocked an opponent down but they aren't dead yet, you can use them to reveal the location of their team mates. Pick them up and shake them down, and you'll see their teammates outlined in red, even if there are solid objects between you and them. It can give you a useful advantage when it comes to tracking them down – but you need to be careful that you don't get eliminated while heading over to the fallen opponent first. ⬇

TACTICS: TEAM RUMBLE

IT'S 50 PLAYERS PER TEAM AND RESPAWNS ARE ON. IT'S FAST AND FURIOUS, SO LOCK AND LOAD AND LET'S GET READY FOR BATTLE!

HARVEST AND OPEN WEAPONS ON YOUR WAY TO THE BATTLE ZONE

Make sure you explore as much ground as you can as quickly as you can when you land. It's even worth staying on the Battle Bus a little longer to grab weapons from further afield, giving you a wider choice. While uncommon and higher weapons are dropped when a player is shot, it pays to start with as strong a selection of weapons as you can! ⬆

WORK IN TEAMS IF YOU CAN

With 50 strangers on each side, formulating any kind of clear tactical approach can be absolute mayhem. In fact, it's pretty much impossible. You'll find it much more fruitful if you can jump into a squad with one, two or three of your buddies and join a 50-a-side team that way. At least you'll be able to work cohesively as a smaller group and help each other out. ➡

HELP YOUR WEAKER MEMBERS

It may become clear in the battle that some players on your team are struggling with their weapons payload – they weren't smart enough early on and are paying for it now. If you see that's the case, be generous. You don't need three legendary weapons, for example – give one to a teammate. If they are nothing but cannon fodder because they have rubbish weapons, it'll only impact your own chances of ending on the winning team. ⬆

DEFEND SUPPLY DROPS

Nothing is fought over harder than supply drops in Team Rumble. The goodies inside can be crucial, and whole games can change with an influx of new weapons. Prioritise helping your team dominate the supply drops. Once you know where they are landing, get straight to work building defensive structures around the drop zone from which you and your colleagues can keep the other side from getting the goodies first. ⬆

HEAL WHEN YOU CAN

Knockdowns don't count against you, but eliminations do. That means healing a teammate before they run out of health is just as valuable to your team's score as sniping an opponent with a headshot from 75 metres away. If you see teammates in trouble, help them wherever possible – and be generous when it comes to sharing medkits and shield potions. It's all for the greater good, remember. ⬇

PLAY THE ODDS

Sometimes, it just isn't your day. If you're having one of those games where you keep getting taken out, can't find a decent weapon to save your life and it all seems to be going wrong – stay out of the way. Stick to the edges of the battle, trying to avoid the heaviest fighting until you can get your hands on a decent weapon that evens the odds a little bit. ⬇

LIFE ON THE EDGE

With so many players, combat can be really chaotic so, if you do get shot and need to respawn, try to land on the edges of the combat zone rather than slap bang in the middle of it. It will give you a little longer to get your bearings, rather than running the risk of you landing directly in front of someone's shotgun barrel. ←

GRENADE LOTTERY

There is no friendly fire in the game, and there are people just about everywhere. If you have plenty of grenades and need some space in your inventory, throwing a few 'Hail Marys' into the epicentre of a battle is a great idea. You won't hurt your own players, but you will cause damage to the opponents they are fighting against so it's always worth taking a chance! →

BUILDING AND EXTENDING

Often, Team Rumble games rest on building in the middle of the area. If your team has a building going, play your part in adding to it and/or repairing it as best you can. If you're starting one off early on in the game, try to build out from an existing structure so you already have something of a height advantage – that way, there's less work to do. ↓

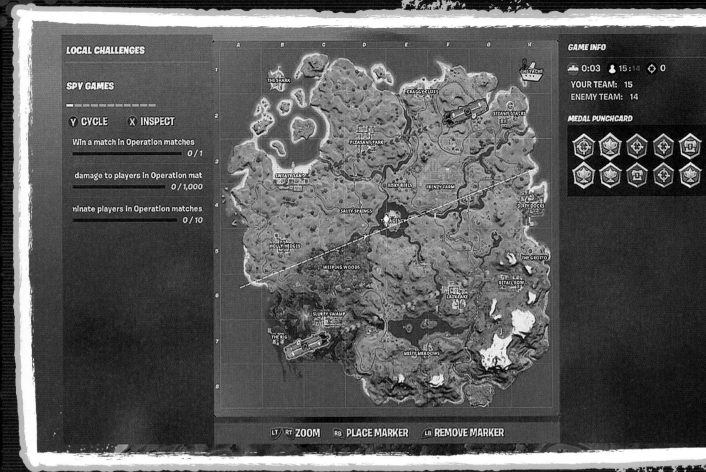

GO WITH THE FLOW

Because both teams start at opposite ends of the island, there's usually a battle line drawn somewhere in the middle. Try and stick to your team's side of it. That will mean your opponents are largely in front of you, giving you more chance of racking up the kills without being flanked. Going lone wolf in this game mode is a recipe for disaster, as you'll be picked off in next to no time. ⬆

VEHICLE ADVANTAGE

The various vehicles that are available in Fortnite (they change over time, but there's usually one or two) can be game changers, especially if you load up with teammates for extra firepower. Make claiming them a priority as much as you can, and if you find any on your way to the battle zone, there really is no finer way to announce your arrival... ⬇

COMPLETE CHALLENGES

The sheer volume of players means that Team Rumble is a great opportunity to complete challenges that might take a lot longer in solo mode. It's one of the quickest ways to boost your XP so it's well worth investing some time playing it. For newcomers, it's also a great way to get more bang for your V-Buck – there's no chance of being blasted with a shotgun as soon as you land and finding yourself the first player out of the game. Instead, you can be sure of a fast and furious fighting experience! ⬆

OFF THE BEATEN TRACK

THE FORTNITE ISLAND IS PACKED WITH LOCATIONS, BUT AT THE BIGGER PLACES YOU CAN OFTEN FIND YOURSELF IN A FAST AND FURIOUS GUNFIGHT FROM THE VERY START AS EVERYONE COMPETES FOR RESOURCES IN THE SAME AREAS.

I f you want to be a little more cunning than your rivals, the smart move is always to land at a location that ISN'T on the map. Newer players won't know about them and you can often find yourself able to stock up on weapons and resources in complete solitude before heading to a bigger location nearby to get involved with the action. **Here are some of our favourite places to land for a quieter start to your Battle Royale.**

LAKE CANOE

Map location: G5

Lake Canoe is found to the north of Retail Row, and is one of the best places to drop outside of the named locations. It's home to a collection of buildings around a central lake (which is also home to an island). If you see anyone else heading towards the areas, it's big enough that you can drop in a different house and load up with weapons before moving over to take them out, while you are reasonably central when it comes to moving on should the storm circle require you too. There are loot chests in most of the buildings, and often on the central island too.

The buildings offer excellent cover and good vantage points should anyone start moving into the area once you are in position. It's a pretty simple location to defend, with the flexibility of offering an escape route in any direction if you do find yourself overrun at any point. A perfect place to start your Fortnite game more often than not!

APRÉS SKI

Map location: E8

Located near the top of a mountain, Aprés Ski used to be a real hot drop, but it's largely forgotten by lots of Fortnite gamers these days. You can use that to your advantage, however, as there are a couple of loot chests to be had. It also offers the great advantage of high ground should you decide to bed down and play a defensive game where you sit tight and let your opponents come to you.

If you do decide to move on, Misty Meadows is immediately to the north and you can reach it easily enough by dropping down the mountain. Alternatively, if you find yourself coming under too much heat, you can always escape by leaping into the sea to the south – provided the storm circle is favourable and you'll have time to swim to a new part of the map!

HOMELY HILLS

Map location: C1, C2, D1, D2

Homely Hills is a well-heeled, nice part of the island home to nice houses with well-kept yards and lots of room. Unfortunately, you'll be smashing the place apart pretty quickly to harvest resources and gather weapons.

Located to the north, Frenzy Farm, Pleasant Park and Steamy Stacks are likely to be competing with each other to be your next destination. The five houses in Homely Hills are quite well spread out (posh people need lots of space, don't you know) which can work to your favour if you have company as you come in to land – you can head a quiet house, tool up and then start hunting!

There are plenty of loot chests to get you off to a good start, and the sea to the north can provide a useful escape route if your early position is overrun. That said, the various buildings mean that it's also a good location to defend, with the option of dropping back to another house and leaving some traps behind you if you face a few

WEATHER STATION

Map location: In the south of G7

Another reasonably well-known location, the Weather Station has enough loot chests to keep you happy and well stocked from the start. Because it's quite a remote choice of initial landing spot, it often is quite quiet so you're unlikely to find much in the way of competition for the weaponry there, and you can then get busy harvesting the building itself for resources without worrying about unwanted attention.

Your next port of call will probably be moving north towards either Lazy Lake or Retail Row, though you can move west towards Misty Meadows if you'd rather.

FARMERS MARKET

Map location: In the north of F3

This building and surrounding buildings is a really good landing location, just to the north of Frenzy Farm. Most players in the area will rush to Frenzy Farm, which means you will most likely have your pick of the considerable loot chests dotted around the main building and in the surrounding outbuildings. You'll often find goodies in the orchards surrounding the buildings too.

When the time comes to move on, another benefit reveals itself – you're pretty central. You have the option of moving to most parts of the map fairly quickly without having to cover vast expanses. Depending on what the storm circle is doing, there's often some value in sitting tight though, as players from the nearby locations may well have to pass through or nearby as they flee the storm. When they do so, you can be there, armed to the teeth and ready for them!

GORGEOUS GORGE

Map location: Running through the middle of E5 to F5

Gorgeous Gorge is not exactly a hotspot for buildings and loot chests – though you will still be able to find a pretty decent set of weapons fairly quickly. However, this is a landing spot that's all about its central location. If you're not the kind of player who likes having to move long distances and you prefer instead to be settled and pretty much guaranteed to be in the storm circle from the start, Gorgeous Gorge is the place for you.

Lazy Lakes and Frenzy Farm are very close to the gorge, so you can be in either of those locations within a couple of minutes. It gives you a good amount of flexibility when it comes to choosing your route, and it's also a good back up option if your initial plan was to land in one of those locations but they looked too hot on arrival.

FORT CRUMPET

Map location: Middle of A3

Sweaty Sands is an increasingly busy landing zone in Fortnite, so landing there can be a risky business. However, a short trot away is a place where you can land in peace, stock up with weapons, harvest all the stone you could ever dream of, and then sweep through and mop up the survivors in Sweaty Sands.

We're talking about Fort Crumpet, a disused fort that is home to plenty of loot chests. It's in a fairly isolated position out to the west of the map, so your only way out is to head south towards Sweaty Sands, but you should be so well provided for weapons-wise that this isn't a major concern.

Depending on where the storm circle heads early on, it can also be an excellent place to sit in and use as a defensive stronghold (funny that, with it being a castle). It's a good place to fortify with a few extra structures of your own, especially if you are playing Duos or Squads – you can really go to town with it.

SHIPWRECK COVE

Map location: South of H7

This drop zone is one of the most secluded places on the map, situated in the bottom right of the map. It's separated from Retail Row and Lazy Lake by the mountains, and you have only the sea to your back.

That does make it a bit of a gamble – although there are loot chests to be found here, if you don't get decent weapons in them then you are a long way from anywhere else and might find yourself up against it. On the plus side, it's a secluded enough area and you can always grab a boat or swim around the coast towards Retail Row if the mountains are looking a bit too much of a risk.

MOUNT F8

Map location: F8

Another great location to land in due to the fact that it occupies high ground is the abandoned camp at Mount F8. As well as being on high ground, thus giving you an immediate advantage, it's also in a good location between Mount Kay and the southernmost weather station.

That location makes it an ideal back-up choice if you are heading to one of these other locations but discover you're going to be late to a busy party. It's home to loot chests and ammo boxes, and you should be able to get together enough weaponry to launch an attack on the weather station or Mount Kay straight away.

If neither of those options appeals, then you can just slip down the mountain towards Lazy Lake to the north west. In any case, the lack of buildings here means that it's not somewhere to sit and defend – there's not much to harvest and nowhere to hide.

MOUNT KAY

Map location: G7

Another abandoned mountain encampment, there's very little to choose between Mount Kay and Mount F8. There are no real structures to speak of, other than flimsy tents, but again you will benefit from the advantage of high ground should you come under attack early on in the game. There are enough loot chests and ammo boxes in the area to get you off to a solid start, and you can then move on to your next destination depending on where the storm circle sends you.

Mount Kay is a fair way south, however, so you can find yourself putting in a long old run to make it to the northern parts of the map if you're unlucky with the first storm circle, so keep an eye on where it forms and don't waste time if you need to get moving.

COUNTRY HOUSE

Map location: North of E6

This white wooden house is in a valley, with higher ground on all sides, so its not somewhere to spend too much time. However, it does sit in a very secluded part of the map with no landmarks especially near it, so it's often a quiet place to drop.

It's bountiful too, with loot chests in the house (including usually in the loft) and you'll have plenty of time to get your weapons together before deciding where you want to attack next.

The roof does give a decent line of sight of the surrounding area to help you spot anyone coming for you, but because of those nearby hills and peaks, you are usually better off moving on once you've ransacked the place.

LOCKIE'S LIGHTHOUSE

Map location: Middle of C1

Well, if you want views for days then a lighthouse is always going to give you a great vantage point. From here, you'll be able to see anyone approaching you so if you're a good shot from distance, you can defend yourself quite easily. There are plenty of loot chests in the lighthouse itself, too. If you opt to drop here, you can usually land on the top of the lighthouse easily enough then nip down a couple of floors to grab a loot chest or two, meaning you can start picking off opponents pretty quickly.

If you want more weapons, there's a house on the same hill too, which is home to more loot chests so you can head south and into combat well and truly tooled up!

NORTHERN WEATHER STATION

Map location: North of F2

This weather station, abandoned by henchmen at the end of Chapter 2 Season 2, is in a very useful location in the northern section of the map. Firstly, and most importantly, it's got loot chests inside that you can use to ensure you are well armed from the off. However, it is also an excellent vantage point from which you can see enemies approaching from any direction, making it a great place to set up to defend in Squads or Duos.

As well as being a sniper's dream, it's also handily placed for other destinations you might want to

STUMPY RIDGE

Map location: D6

Stumpy Ridge might not seem like much to write home about – after all, it consists of little more than a few tree stumps and some trucks loaded and ready to haul the logs away.

However, that peace and tranquillity is one of the benefits of Stumpy Ridge. Very few gamers ever land there, and there's a loot chest and a reasonable smattering of weapons in the area to help get you started. The wood loaded onto the trucks is also a useful to harvest and will give you enough for your early building needs. You're in a reasonably central location too, with Aprés Ski within easy reach if you want to claim some higher ground.

OLD SAFE HOUSE

Map location: D5

This abandoned former safe house is an excellent starting point now the henchmen are no longer around to make your life hell. It's absolutely chock full of loot chests and ammo boxes, and is large enough for you to knock down internal walls to harvest materials without leaving yourself exposed to an attack from nearby.

If the storm circle favours you and you don't have to move, its also an excellent location to defend, especially in Squads or Duos. From the rooftop you'll be able to see anyone approaching from the north or west – the only area to really worry about is anyone attacking from the east, as the mountains behind you mean they'll have the high ground. Of course, if that happens, you can simply use the building as cover and wait for them to come to you, then pick them off once they've had to surrender their advantage in order to come and find you...

RAPIDS REST

Map location: In the west of G6

There are definitely more exciting places to land than Rapid's Rest, but it does offer a handy escape point between Retail Row and Lazy Lake if you find yourself coming into land in either of those locations but things look a bit too hot to handle for you.

It's basically just a little boating site on the river, but you'll usually find a weapon inside the hut and a loot chest in the rocks on the river itself. There's also a motorboat in among all the kayaks that you can leap into if you need to get away from the area quickly. If you're feeling a little braver, you can head on to Retail Row (to the east) or Lazy Lake (pretty much immediately to the west).

FERRIS BUELLER'S HOUSE

Map location: Middle of A4

This house is modelled on the house from Ferris Bueller's day off – a modern looking, split level residence complete with a smashed up Ferrari being rescued by crane. If you don't know the film, stop reading now, go and watch it, then come back and pick up where you left off – it's a classic.

Back with us? Good. There are usually weapons on the roof and loot chests inside the house (check downstairs!). Once you've grabbed everything you need from the house itself, you'll often find loot chests on or near the crane, and heading north will take you to a secluded cover with shipping containers where you can pick up a decent selection of weapons too.

Once you're ready to move out, there are two locations – Sweaty Sands (which can often be quite busy) to the north east, and Holly Hedges to the south east.

H SHAPED HOUSE

Map location: In the south of A4

This location is quite near Ferris Bueller's House (well that's what we're calling it) so it's quite easy to visit them both in a single visit. It's well worth the diversion too, as it is home to loot chests inside and out as well as offering decent views of the surrounding area from the upstairs windows and roof.

What's more, you'll also find an upgrade bench in the house so you can upgrade a weapon or two if you can gather enough resources. It's nice and close to Sweaty Sands too, so you can push on and cause some mischief there once you're ready to throw yourself into some combat

GAS 'N' GRUB

Map location: In the north of F5

Everyone knows gas stations are a great place to stock up on treats, and this one is no different! It's in a pretty secluded location between Frenzy Farm to the north and Lazy Lake to the south, so it's rarely home to lots of players early on in the game, but many will pass through it as the storm circle shrinks. That makes it a good place to sit and lie in wait having opened the loot chests that it is home to and picked up the weapons dotted around the place.

Don't forget to search the adjoining diner thoroughly too – there are usually more goods to be had there.

SURVIVING THE END GAME

IF YOU'VE MADE IT DOWN TO BE ONE OF THE LAST FIVE PLAYERS STANDING, THEN CONGRATULATIONS – YOU'VE ALREADY DONE A GREAT JOB! WANT TO TURN THAT INTO A VICTORY ROYALE? YOU'LL BE NEEDING THESE TIPS THEN!

HAVE PLENTY OF MATERIALS
The Victory Royale almost always goes to players that can build well. You need to have mastered building already (see page 64 for more!) otherwise the odds are you'll be out built and out thought! That means you need decent supplies of materials as you enter the final stages which in turn means planning for success starts early! Harvest what you can from the start of the game, especially metal and brick – you'll thank yourself later when you can build structures that withstand a beating from your final few opponents. ⬆

KNOW YOUR ENEMY

Keep an eye on the feed on your HUD. It tells you who has killed who in the game and can help you understand who your likely opponents will be towards the end of the game. It can be useful to know if you are facing players ranked in the 150s or 200s, or if the final few opponents are much lower ranked. It's also useful to know how they are making their kills, which also shows up on the HUD. Knowing whether there's a sniper in the ranks at the end of the game can be a vital early warning. ⬇

HEAL THYSELF

Once there are only a few players left and the storm circle is tiny, it's highly unlikely you'll have the ten seconds you need to put that medkit to use. You are far better off with large shield potions instead, so from around the last 20 or so, think ahead and ditch medkits in favour of shield potions. They're quicker to use and you'll be vulnerable for a much shorter timeframe. ⬇

PAYLOAD PERFECTION

The ideal loadout for an endgame will vary depending on your tactics, but it's advisable to have a few different options open to you. A shotgun for close range combat should be con-sidered essential, along with some form of healing item – shield potions are the best here, but medpacks will do if not. Next up you'll want some form of explosive. A rocket launcher with plenty of ammo is definitely the dream here, but if not then grenades or other explo-sives will just have to do. The standard assault rifle or a similar mid-range item is another must-have. Your fifth and final item should be something that fits in with your preferred tactics – another grenade slot to give yourself 12 in total can be handy. As a rule, the sniper rifle isn't the most effective in the frenetic pace of the end game, so that's one we'd advise leaving behind. If you've found a minigun, however, then that should make your mind up for you! ⬆

STORMING A FORT

If you find yourself in a situation where you need to storm someone else's fort in the final two, it's always worth remembering that very few players build roofs on their structures. There are two different ways you can take advantage of this particular scenario. Firstly, you can lob grenades up over the walls. Spread them out so you have more chance of them hit-ting your opponent with at least one of them – the damage from the inside might also cause part of the fort to collapse, leaving them exposed and vulnerable.

If you don't have grenades then simply build a staircase up and over their fort then either look down and shoot them or drop in and finish them from close range with a shotgun. ⬇

LOOK BUT DON'T TOUCH

If you're down to the last three and you see your other two opponents fighting with each other, get as close as you can as quickly as you can, but DON'T FIRE! You'll draw attention to yourself and they might both turn on you. Instead, wait for one to eliminate the other and quickly turn your attention to the survivor who will hopefully have taken a few hits in the fight and have lower health as a result. Before they can heal, you should be able to land some further damage that will be enough to finish them off! ⬆

STAIRWAY TO HEAVEN

If you find yourself in a shootout with an opponent from relatively close quarters, get the high ground as quickly as you can – build a small stone staircase, two or three units high, with a flat floor tile at the end, as you are running towards them. Use the high ground to take them out before they can build a fort to defend themselves! ⬇

AIR TIME

Using launchpads or crash pads can be a great way to leap into an enemy fort, so if you have one in your inventory towards the end of the game, use it. They can also be a valuable asset in your own construction – if you have time to build two forts and then leap from one to the other you can get the edge on your opponents but this is quite complicated to achieve! ⬆

CAUGHT IN A TRAP

The small space in the end of the game means people are moving quickly so if you have proximity mines or any kind of traps, drop them around the map and then fill the empty inventory space with something that is more immediately useful. There's a good chance in the mayhem of the closing stages someone will stumble into one and do themselves some damage. They might even win you the game! ⬇

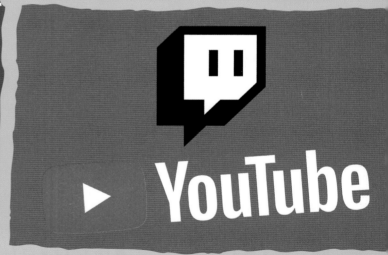

LOOK AND LEARN

If you really want to learn how the best Fortnite players win at endgame, watch their YouTube or Twitch channels. By seeing how they deal with different situations, you can come to understand your own game better and begin to have some different tactical responses ready. ⬆

BUILDING

BEING A CRACK SHOT WITH AN ASSAULT RIFLE WILL ONLY GET YOU SO FAR IN FORTNITE! TO TRULY MASTER THE GAME, YOU'LL NEED TO BE ABLE TO BUILD SUCCESSFULLY TOO – SO HERE'S OUR GUIDE TO EVERYTHING YOU NEED TO KNOW!

MASTER YOUR MATERIALS

You'll need a mix of material types throughout the game, so harvest wood, brick and metal. Even the three little pigs knew that stronger materials are better, so you'll need to use the right material for the right purpose. Using metal to build a ramp up to a mountain is a waste of resources, as is constructing a defensive structure from wood when you are inside the final storm circle with only a handful of players remaining.

As a rule, use wood for most things in the early part of the game because the odds are you will have to move on as the storm circle closes. Once you are into the last five or so, you can start to think about constructing something a little more substantial!

PRACTICE MAKES PERFECT

Even a simple structure can be tough to build in the middle of a game, when you're under fire from an opponent or the storm is closing in on you. The more complicated structures like forts take even more time to master. The answer is simple – head to creative mode and practice. Train yourself to build the structures you'll learn about in this section so in-stinctively that you don't even have to think about it. That way, when you need to do it for real you'll be much quicker to get things in place

THE HEALING SHED

Ideally, try and heal up somewhere already sheltered – by nipping into a nearby building, for example, or hiding in a bush. It's not always possible, however. Sometimes, you'll sustain damage in a long-distance firefight and be so low on health that you can't risk another player landing a shot on you. In those situations, construct a simple 1x1 square around yourself and stick a roof on (to protect against grenades or enemies with higher ground). Once inside your structure, you can drink some shield potion or apply bandages without running the risk of being sniped from a distance. You can also do this as a sniping point – it's called turtling (because you're safe in your shell!)

OUTRUN THE STORM

If the storm is closing in on you and you're trying to run to safety, your plans can be seriously compromised by an inconvenient mountain in the way. You'd be amazed how many players lose precious time and health by skirting around the mountain when it's far easier to build a ramp up to it so you can scale it in seconds. Once you've done this, turn around and try to shoot the bottom out (if you have time) to save anyone running from the storm who happens to be behind you doing the same thing!

ATTACK FROM ABOVE

If you know a building contains opponents, entering in the conventional manner (ie via the door) can be lethal — they may well have the doors covered, or have planted explosives near them. Instead, surprise them from above — build a quick ramp to the top floor or roof and either drop down through an existing opening or smash through yourself to completely change the angle of attack. This can be a useful approach in squads or duos too, splitting a coordinated attack so that you hit your opponents from above and below at the same time.

THE SNIPING TOWER

This is perhaps the staple of Fortnite building. Practice and practice it until you can do it in your sleep. Stand still, then spin round, building four walls as you do to close yourself in. Then jump into the air and, while airborne, build some stairs. You'll land on them and can walk to the top. Once there, repeat the process, building four walls on top of the four you just built, jumping and building

another staircase. Repeating this four or five times can give you a nice tall tower from where you can look out for approaching enemies and, if you have a sniper rifle or are a crack shot with the assault rifle, pick them off.

Don't build it too tall though, because a smart opponent can blow out the bottom of it and send you crashing to your doom.

THE EXTENSION

Why do all the hard work yourself? Sometimes it can save a lot of time and effort to occupy an existing structure on the island and build onto it. The existing structures tend to have much sturdier walls too, so you can get the best of both worlds – a structure high enough for outstanding vantage points that can't be smashed down easily.

As well as adding your own construction to an existing building, you can also simply modify one. For example, you could smash out a section of wall on the top floor then immediately replace it with your own wall, into which you insert a window. You now have a fantastic sniping hideyhole that took just a few seconds to construct!

THE SPRAWLING FORT

This is where things get serious! These are best built very late in the game, where the storm circle is small enough for you to be sure you'll get good value for it. It's absolutely guaranteed that you will come under attack, so make it out of metal and brick. However, at this stage of the game, it's time to abandon the simple approach of the 1x1 sniper tower – it's too easy for an opponent to find you with a shot from a rocket launcher or a grenade.

Constructing a fort means you need to think laterally – build sideways as well as upward so that you have room to leap around inside. Throw in ramps and walls in more than one direction to keep your opponents guessing where you are, and make the most of the edit function to place windows to shoot from before editing them back again before they return fire!

The key is not to stand still and to keep throwing up new parts of the structure, moving as fast as you can to keep your opponent disoriented.

CHOOSE YOUR OWN ADVENTURE

ONE OF THE COOLEST THINGS IN FORTNITE IS THE CHANCE TO CREATE YOUR OWN GAME, FOLLOWING YOUR RULES, *JUST THE WAY YOU LIKE IT.* YOU CAN THEN INVITE FRIENDS TO JOIN YOU AND SEND YOUR UNIQUE ISLAND CODE OUT SO ANYONE CAN PLAY IT! *HERE'S THE KEY THINGS YOU NEED TO KNOW!*

LOOK AND LEARN

It's worth checking out islands that other people have created. Designing your own island is not easy – there's a reason why the best games designers in the world get paid to do it! You can find some great examples to get you started on page 72. Try a few different game types, and check out what's popular in the Creative Hub. You'll soon get a feel for the kind of games you like playing and the kind of games you aren't so keen on, which will help you decide on the best way to approach your own challenge. You'll also learn what works well in the Fortnite world and what's not so good to play, which will help you design your own challenges. ⬅

CLEAR INSTRUCTIONS

Include clear instructions for anyone who is going to play your game. There's nothing more frustrating then landing on someone else's island and everything looking really cool, but you have no idea how to play it, what you are meant to do, or where you are supposed to go next. Don't be too ambitious or get too clever too quickly – start with simple steps and work your way up to more complex concepts. →

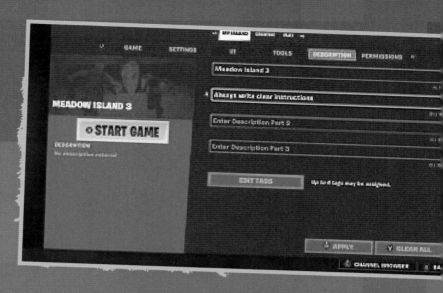

PREFABS

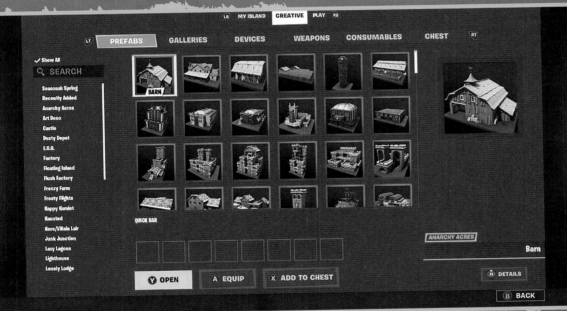

Inside the prefabs menu, you'll find all of the assets used in the game itself along with some extra buildings you can make the most of. It'll take you a long time to look through it all, but it is worth getting to know what you have available to you so you can use them properly. ←

USE THE GRID

Placing things freestyle suits some players, but it's often easier to plan a level properly if you use a grid. This option is turned off to start with, but you can change that using the Grid Snap option. There are three different settings for the sizes between objects, from right next to each other to quite a distance away, so experiment with this until you get the gaps you want. ↓

DRAW IT OUT

It sounds silly, but it can be hard to picture what you want to create when you're actually in the game. Sometimes, it's best to do these things old school and get some paper! Graph paper can be particularly useful when it comes to figuring out the distances to leave between buildings.

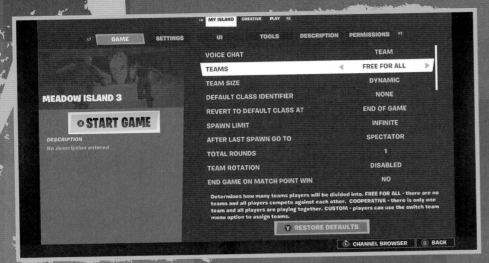

CHOOSE YOUR RULES

Inside the My Island menu you'll find all the options that you can change. This includes all of the rules for the game – the game mode, team sizes, time limits, spawn locations and more can be edited here. ←

MERGING STRUCTURES

You can choose to turn clipping on or off in the menu, which will decide whether buildings will 'merge' when you place one on top of the other. This can be a great way to create unique structures on your island without spending hours and hours building them from scratch. →

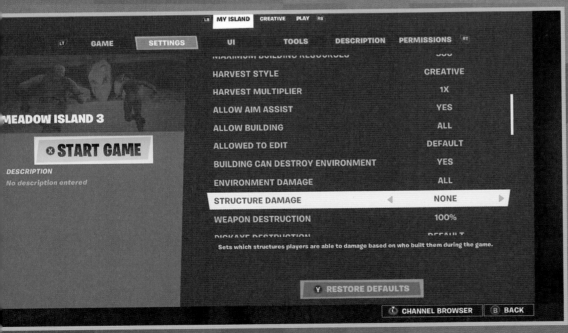

USE A COMPUTER

Generally, it's a bit easier to make your own island using a laptop so, if you have a PC or laptop, use that instead – even if you usually play on a games console. You can install the game and use your existing login details; it's just a lot quicker using a mouse or trackpad than it is using a game controller!

UNBREAKABLE

If you need your players to head in a certain direction or do something specific, the best way to do that is to build unbreakable walls so that they realise which direction they are meant to be heading in – otherwise people could be ambling around your level design for ages! ↑

DON'T LET PEOPLE MESS!

When you're finished with your world, remember to turn the editing lock on. If you don't, then other players will be able to mess with your creation once they enter it. If you want to find it as you left it, make sure you lock it down! ➡

BACK IT UP!

You wouldn't write a huge essay for school or a report for work and not save it as you went along, would you? Do the same with your Fortnite island! There's nothing more annoying than spending hours working on a really cool game only for a power cut to cost you the whole thing. On the same note, always save it before you try adding something especially complicated in, so you can go back to how it was to start with if your experiment doesn't work. And lastly, create a backup of your island too, so if your save corrupts you've got something you can rebuild it from! ⬅

WHAT'S IN THE CHEST

You're in control of what's available in each loot chest, remember. You can use that to add interesting twists to your game, but try to make it reasonably fair and make sure that the better weapons are evenly spread out. Alternatively, you could use what is in each loot chest as part of the mechanics for your game.

For example, you could make pistols the only available weapon, or sniper rifles. You could decide not to include any medkits or shield potions so that damage really counts. The possibilities are endless, and the choices are all yours! ⬇

I BELIEVE I CAN FLY!

It sounds obvious, but don't forget you can fly around the map in Creative mode. If you're working on a big, sprawling environment for a large deathmatch then it can take ages to be walking between your different buildings and settlements. Using the flying mode allows you to move much quicker, but it also lets you see things from a different perspective, helping you to make sure that your map is well balanced and fair! ⬆

CHOOSE YOUR OWN

The ability to build your own Fortnite world in Creative mode and then open it out to other gamers is one of the most awesome parts of the Fortnite community. There are some seriously talented people out there looking at Fortnite in different and creative ways. Here are some of the best fan-created game modes out there. To play them, go to one of the consoles by a portal in Creative mode and enter the code. Because some of these are older games, you're unlikely to find them teeming with players though, so to make the most of the fun, squad up with some friends to play the maps.

If you enjoy any of these maps, remember to support the creator – they get a little kick back from Epic when you buy things from the store that way, and it gives them encouragement to keep making amazing game modes!

SNIPERS VS RUNNERS

Creator: BluDrive **Code:** 6352-8048-2222

It's such a simple idea for a game, but like many simple ideas, it works brilliantly. One team are runners. The other team are snipers. The team of runners are challenged to complete a parkour-type obstacle course in five minutes or less, which sounds simple enough. However, the other team has a much more sinister objective.

Armed with sniper rifles, their job is to knock the runners off their intended route or eliminate them, losing them valuable time. The game is more than just a standalone effort though – it's actually a brilliant training exercise in getting you accustomed to moving and jumping, while also helping you to master the sniper rifle against moving opponents – probably one of the hardest Fortnite skills.

ADVENTURE!

MODERN WARFARE 2: SHIPMENT

Creator: benz4ducks **Code:** 4804-9489-3873
Another Modern Warfare 2 favourite, Shipment is a legendary map because of the fast-paced and frenetic nature. A tiny map set inside a small yard full of shipping containers, you never know where an opponent is going to leap out from and blast you.

It's definitely a level where you can forget about using a sniper rifle – shotguns and assault rifles are the order of the day here. Stealth can help you secure a few kills but to really ramp things up you'll need to throw yourself into the frantic feel of the map and charge around like a mad thing. If you've not played it before, you'll quickly see why it was such a favourite with Modern Warfare 2 fans!

MODERN WARFARE 2: TERMINAL

Creator: xlp629 **Code:** 6412-7533-9638
The idea of taking classic levels from other games and building them in a different title is not a new one, but this version of the classic Terminal map from Call of Duty: Modern Warfare 2 is inspired. The attention to detail is incredible, with every area of the map faithfully recreated. Perhaps the biggest challenge was the plane sitting on the tarmac – many an old-school gamer will have very fond memories of trying to storm that!

With no planes available in the Fortnite building blocks, creator xlp629 has shown remarkable creativity in reconstructing a plane out of the materials that are available. The result is a level that's great for some 1v1 battles, with open spaces for combat, good sniping vantage points, and lots of places to hide and sneak up on your opponent.

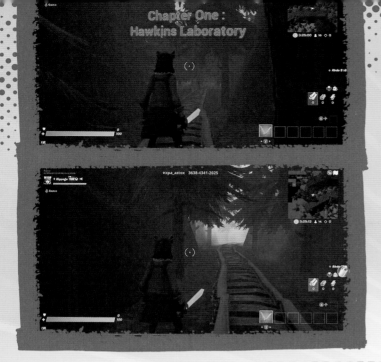

HAWKINS LABORATORY FROM STRANGER THINGS

Creator: Expa_aztox Code: 3638-4341-2025
We LOVED Stranger Things on Netflix, so we thought we'd give this Fortnite tie-in a whirl too. What we probably love about it most, is the way that Expa_aztox has managed to capture the spirit of the series so well. The dark woods around the laboratory in eerie moonlight, coupled with the mist that inhibits how far you can see really makes you feel as if you're there in the TV series.

There's even a pretty decent stab at the theme music too. It's a fun experience to play through the challenge so, if you liked the series, give it a go!

RAINBOW SIX SIEGE: HOUSE

Creator: Fatal Creations Code: 9315-3255-7086
In keeping with enjoying playing levels from other games that Fortnite gamers have recreated, this map from Rainbow Six Seige is one of the best out there. It looks just like the real thing and every aspect of the gameplay has been thought through in real detail.

There's a wide variety of different characters to play as, and lots of spawn points to choose from. The house itself can be damaged too, just like in Rainbow Six: Seige, so you can breach walls and clear rooms to your heart's content.

The game works like the real thing too, with one team having to defend two bomb points, while the other has to break into the house and defuse the bombs. Absolutely fantastic fun and one map you really shouldn't miss out on!

JURASSIC JUNGLE

Creator: 0KYT **Code:** 0029-6873-5504

This deathrun (basically parkour with a bit more risk) is definitely one of the COOLEST out there because it takes place in Jurassic Park. Yeah that's right – THE Jurassic Park. From the moment you step through those famous double gates, you're in Jurassic Park, moving through dino enclosures and the buildings made famous by the film. It's home to a few soldiers as well, like the guys from Jurassic Park 2.

You'll even bump into a few dinosaurs on your journey, as well as traps and tricky jumps to make. It's a pretty faithful recreation of the park, and highly recommended if you're a Fortnite fan who enjoyed the movies!

TOY STORY

Creator: trizbear **Code:** 5530-6235-0681

This is a prop hunt game, which basically means it's a game of hide and seek where one player disguises themselves as an object in the game, and the others have to find them and destroy their disguise.

This game applies that concept to a really cool place – Andy's bedroom from Toy Story! Trizbear has done a great job of recreating the room, incorporating lots of places to hide and lots of cool nods to Toy Story to disguise yourself as.

There's even an oversized Mr & Mrs Potato Head overseeing the action!

FABULOUS FORTNITE QUIZ!

HOW MUCH ATTENTION HAVE YOU BEEN PAYING? THE ANSWERS TO ALL THESE QUESTIONS ARE SOMEWHERE IN THIS ULTIMATE GUIDE. CAN YOU ANSWER WITHOUT HAVING TO LOOK UP THE ANSWERS?

1 Which one of these film characters is NOT a real Fortnite skin?

a) Rey from Star Wars
b) John Wick
c) Deadpool
d) Judge Dredd

2 Which of these weapons takes the longest time to reload between shots?

a) Pump action shotgun
b) Assault rifle
c) Tactical shotgun
d) SMG

3 What's the maximum number of players you can have on a Fortnite squad?

a) Four
b) Five
c) Six
d) Two

4 Which of these ISN'T a real Fortnite location?

a) Risky Reels
b) Hydro 16
c) Mystery Mansion
d) Sweaty Sands

5 What's the maximum health you can reach using bandages?

a) 100%
b) 75%
c) 80%
d) 50%

6 **Where in the game you improve the quality of your weapon?**

a) Weapon workshop
b) TNT toolshed
c) Upgrade bench
d) Fortnite forge

7 **Which of the following materials CAN'T you build with?**

a) Straw
b) Wood
c) Stone
d) Metal

8 **What does the phrase "loot baiting" mean?**

a) Eliminating someone while they are fishing
b) Using explosives to eliminate an opponent
c) Using weapons and goodies to lure an opponent out from cover
d) Stealing someone's vehicle

9 **In which year did Fortnite launch?**

a) 2017
b) 2016
c) 2000
d) 2020

10 **Which rapper joined Tyler 'Ninja' Blevins on Twitch?**

a) Jay-Z
b) Drake
c) Kanye West
d) Eminem

11 **Which music star held the first online concert in Fortnite?**

a) Marshmello
b) Bruno Mars
c) Justin Bieber
d) Dua Lipa

12 **How much melee damage does your harvesting tool do?**

a) 10
b) 50
c) 80
d) 20

ANSWERS!
Turn the page to find out how you did – are you a Fortnite legend or a total noob?

QUIZ ANSWERS!

IT'S THE MOMENT OF TRUTH! HOW DID YOU GET ON WITH OUR FIENDISH FORTNITE TEST?

THE ANSWERS ARE BELOW!

1	d	4	c	7	a	10	b
2	a	5	b	8	c	11	a
3	a	6	c	9	a	12	d

HOW DID YOU SCORE?

0-3 Common

Oh dear! Nothing much to worry anyone who finds themselves in a Battle Royale with you! When it comes to Fortnite, you're best summed up as one of the default skins. While there's nothing wrong with Jonesy and co, maybe you need to spend a little more time learning your trade and climbing the ladder.

4-6 Rare

Not bad, but not great! You may have stopped making silly noob mistakes like jumping out of towers and eliminating yourself, or forgetting to reload after gun battles, but you still have a long way to go before you can count yourself a true Fortnite master!

7-9 Epic

Close, but not quite a legend! You're definitely one of the better Fortnite players in the game, but there are no prizes for making the top ten every time if you can't turn that into a Victory Royale! Other players should definitely pay you some serious respect though – and a little bit more game time could see you fulfilling your obvious potential!

10-12: Legendary

Wow! You really know your Fortnite stuff! You've got bags of skill, and can probably pop the lid off a slurp potion using a pistol from 50m away. You'll never be lost to the storm, and look set for a long list of Battle Royales! Well done!